Look and Find

Trolls

Sparkle Town • Troll Wedding

Ruby's Hair Salon • Sparkle Town School

Jewel Mine • Troll House • And more!

Illustrations
and Script Development
by Bob Terrio

Illustration Assistant: Gale Terrio

Louis Weber, C.E.O.
Publications International, Ltd.
7373 N. Cicero Avenue
Lincolnwood, Illinois 60646

Permission is never granted for commercial purposes.

Manufactured in U.S.A.

8 7 6 5 4 3 2 1

ISBN 1-56173-898-0

PUBLICATIONS INTERNATIONAL, LTD.

Some trolls live in little villages like the one you see here. This is Sparkle Town, named for the sparkling jewels that the trolls mine in the nearby hills.

Look for these Sparkle Town things.

The taxi

The town jeweler

The constable

The flag

The mayor

The key to the city

Miss Sparkle Town

The town bully

Up in the hills near Sparkle Town is the trolls' secret jewel mine. Here, the trolls mine the beautiful gems they like to wear and use in their homes and village.

The troll miners seem to have missed some stones. Can you find these gems?

This diamond

This aquamarine

This topaz

This sapphire

This emerald

This onyx

This ruby

This amethyst

It's just an average day at Sparkle Town School. Students are learning the trolls' three Ms: Math, Magic, and Mining!
    Look for these trolls at the Sparkle Town School.

Sarah Studyhard

Pamela Pep

Peter Principal

Coach Calisthenic

Timmy Toughguy

Paul Paintbrush

Nina Nurse

Ruby's Hair Salon is the busiest shop in Sparkle Town! Ruby and her assistants—Jewel, Opal, Topaz, Emerald, and Moonstone—know how to work miracles on troll hair.

Can you find these special hair designs in Ruby's Salon?

Corn rows

Pigtails

A flat top

A crew cut

A wedge

A beehive

A French twist

MUD BATH

TAN-A-TROLL

This year the annual Troll Summer Frolics are being held in Sparkle Town. Everyone has turned out to root for the Sparkle Town team. May the best troll win!

Many towns have sent their teams to compete at this year's Summer Frolics. Can you find each team's flag?

Crystal City

Daffodil Town

Emerald Heights

Mount Lily

Butterfly Downs

Snailville

Marigold Park

Pinecone Point

The Sparkle Town Emporium is having a big sale today. Trolls have come from miles around to hunt for bargains.

Can you find these specially priced troll items?

This wig

This tricycle

This doll

This raincoat

This jewelry box

This hat

These shoes

This miner's pick

This miner's lantern

Krystal Karat lives with her family in a big house in Sparkle Town. After supper, things get pretty hairy when the kids finish their homework and get ready for bed.

Can you find Krystal and these other Karat family members?

Krystal

Mr. Karat

Mrs. Karat

Grandma Karat

Grandpa Karat

Uncle Earl

Aunt Pearl

Today is a special day in Sparkle Town. The trolls are celebrating the first day of summer with a carnival. All the kids have the day off from school so that they can join in the fun!

Some of the younger kids have become separated from their parents. Can you find them?

Chip

Dusty

Woody

Rose

Daffodil

Daisy

Rocky

Bluebell

Here comes the bride, with hair big and wide! Here comes the groom, with hair like a broom!

There's no wedding like a troll wedding! Can you find these wedding day things?

The flower girl

The ring bearer

The groom's top hat

The bride's bouquet

Something old

Something new

Something borrowed

Something blue

Go back to the Sparkle Town Emporium. Can you find these other bargains?

- [ ] A rolling pin
- [ ] A scuba-diving suit
- [ ] A tuba
- [ ] A beach ball
- [ ] A skateboard
- [ ] A baby buggy
- [ ] An umbrella
- [ ] A telescope

Since it is nighttime at Krystal's house, go back and look for these "night" things.

- [ ] A night "mare"
- [ ] Florence Nightingale
- [ ] A nightcap
- [ ] A nightclub
- [ ] A goodnight kiss
- [ ] "Knight" fall
- [ ] A night light

Wedding bells aren't the only kinds of bells. Can you find these other "bells" at the troll wedding?

- [ ] A belly dancer
- [ ] Bell bottoms
- [ ] A belly laugh
- [ ] A belly button
- [ ] A belly flop
- [ ] A jingle bell
- [ ] Bluebells
- [ ] A southern belle

Go back to the Troll Summer Frolics and look for these games that only trolls play.

- [ ] The daisy toss
- [ ] The spell cast
- [ ] Mouse racing
- [ ] Gem-cutting
- [ ] Diamond lifting
- [ ] Caterpillar wrestling
- [ ] Tunnel digging
- [ ] The troll vault

Sometimes the trolls find things from the human world in the jewel mine. Go back and look for these things.

- [ ] An ink pen
- [ ] A key
- [ ] A pencil
- [ ] A spoon
- [ ] A needle
- [ ] A ribbon
- [ ] A pair of dice
- [ ] A fork